The Ab

Realize the Power Within You

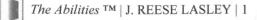

Dedication

"In all your ways, acknowledge Him, and He shall direct your paths." — *Proverbs 3:6*

This book is dedicated to the two most important beings in my life, God and my mother Shana.

The intention of this dedication to God is to help us realize that sometimes, even as hard as we try, our *abilities* are ultimately in His hands. It is His will and His abilities. He is the one who is really in control. He always answers in the right time with the appropriate impact. All our successes are owed unto Him and are because of Him. Therefore, we should work like it depends on us and pray because it depends on God.

I also want to extend this dedication to my mother, who was my source of inspiration for this book. Thank you mom for always being so sweet, so wonderful — and also so strong. You are a miracle and you are my everything.

Table of Contents

Preface

I was raised in a very challenging environment. My mother became terribly sick at a young age and I grew up very quickly. There were many health conditions that she had such as atypical trigeminal neuralgia (ATN), pain medicine addiction, breast cancer, broken bones, strokes, comas, memory loss, hearing loss – and more. She even died and was brought back to life several times. My mother lost everything, including her profession, her friends, her marriage, her house. She was living in a nursing home at age forty-two. The family supported her as much as we could. She experienced unusual hardships in her life, and she didn't have a good quality of life for over twenty-five years.

There hasn't been a sweeter person to walk the earth, and I mean that with all my heart. She didn't deserve any of it. It wasn't her fault. My mom was dealt a joker hand.

Today, she is alive, well and striving. She has overcome breast cancer and her addiction. Her strokes astonishingly cured her ATN, and she is an absolute miracle. They say you truly live life three times: when you are born, when you realize you are going to die and when you go to heaven. I have seen my mother find her life again.

I learned what really mattered in life by helping my mom live her life. My culture and environment gave me a reason to provide and to protect, and the choices I made, given the adversity I faced, afforded me the opportunity to grow. As I grew, while helping my mom live, I decided I wanted to live the best quality of life I could personally. I didn't want the suffering. I didn't want the hardships. I got tired of the destructive behavior, the destitutions of human nature and the sin. I wanted something better. I guess I had a choice to let the adversity defeat me or overcome it. I chose to overcome it.

In other words, through the difficulty, I learned what I needed to do to make a positive difference, and I gained a resilience to pain. I chose to do everything in my power to live life to the fullest. I wanted to succeed, to defeat the status quo, to experience blessings. I wanted happiness, prosperity and health. So, I set out to get what I wanted.

Needless to say, I was never handed resources like some others I knew. However, I learned I didn't need them. I spread my wings. I found a selfless pride in being able to make the sacrifice to take care of myself and others. In fact, in many cases, even if I was offered resources, I chose to earn it for myself. I wanted to be the exception, the extraordinary, the one who overcame.

Over time, I found that my engrained "live the best quality of life possible" personality trait rubbed off on everyone else around me. I looked for opportunities, and what I found on my journey is that inevitably I gained a great deal of wisdom from helping others. I tapped into others' abilities and that made me stronger. Gratefully, they helped me by me helping them. I focused on any way that I could grow and help others grow as well. I built constructive environments and found sincere happiness in this.

If you are anything like me, however, there have been times you have felt frustrated on your journey because you've lacked resources to help others. You feel that you should have a larger impact on humanity, a further reach and be living for something greater.

That is exactly how this book came about. It's my desire to extend my reach into the world. I want to give people *the abilities* to achieve what they want. I find sincere happiness in helping others reach their goals and I want to see other people succeed - in all walks of life. In other words, after reading this book, I hope you find your power within, and truly live.

While I was in the process of writing this book, I was actually diagnosed with testicular cancer. I was reminded of my mother, and I was empowered to overcome. But, personally, I had a conspicuous awakening. Three questions came to mind when I was diagnosed: Am I going to live, will I have the ability to have children, and what can I do now to live life to the fullest? Above everything else I could think of to fulfill my life, I wanted get this book to the world as fast as I could. I decided to share my testimony and hope it helps others live strong. This book was the best outlet to do that.

I find it amazing when people create, take action to execute their hopes and dreams, and strive for what they really want out of life. I believe the people who actually take that chance are the ones finding their true potential. Those who don't, just live to get by. If you live for purpose, however, you will be one of those who finds success.

Therefore, I want to help *you* live life to the fullest and leave a legacy — one that *you* can be proud of.

After reading this book, if you feel like you are experiencing something you need help with, or if your life was influenced, please join our movement. We all have the abilities to leave a mark on this world.

Feel free to reach out to me at reese@theabilities.com, visit our website theabilities.com or share your story on our social media outlets.

Foreword

Children are often asked, "What do you want to be when you grow up?" And with all that imagination, they reply, "A doctor, lawyer, merchant, chief, rich man, poor man, beggar man, thief."

"What do you want to be?" a boy asked a man. The man chuckled and replied with an open heart, "A child again. To dream the dreams of childhood. To see the visions of far shores and trees, for I am a man with a dream fulfilled, and I am not complete. I've sung the songs, I've played the tunes. My heart has felt the beat. I felt the flutter of a butterfly wing against my summer cheek. If now I am asked 'what will you be?' I will be it all. I will climb more mountains, I will cross more creeks. My hands will touch the sky. I will sing, I will build, I will share my love, all before I die.

So, if now I am asked 'what will you be?' I will be it all. More dreams to fill, for I am not complete. You see, boy, I had a nightmare I died last night, early morn. I'm really torn. We hit the ground, then heard a *splash, it was all over in an instant flash. My heart was bleeding, my pulse felt faint. Hard time breathing, happy I ain't. What does this mean, this saddened dream? It means we must start living, we must daydream. Now I am spending the day, happy, and in peace. My first day of living, my first day of living this life on a lease. Borrowed time is what I have left now, so I will make a difference, God make me see how. How to live, how to love, how to be a better me. How to share, how to laugh, to show the world how to see. I want to live a life healthy, pure and strong, I want to live this life, healthy, pure and long. 'Today is the first day of the rest of your life,' a wise man once preached. That day is today, that day I have reached.*

So, God, color my world with a dream of strength, with a vision to see the farthest of length. Strengthen my hands and my courage as well. Don't be a jailer and lock me in a cell. I'm striving to stretch, I gave up my shy. Now I can see where eagles do fly. If I am to die while climbing this task, I did it my best; God told me, I asked. He said, 'I will be your guiding light. Don't hunt after trouble, but look for success! You'll find what you look for, don't look for distress. If you see but your shadow, remember this and pray. The sun is still shining, but you're in the way. Don't grumble, don't bluster, don't gripe, don't shirk. I will take care of you, just think of your work. The worries will vanish, the work will be done, for no man sees his shadow who faces the sun."'

— *Shana Sue Green, my beautiful mother*

Introduction

Everybody wants something. Everybody is giving it the best of their abilities. But do they really have the abilities to get what they want?

There are many definitions, insights and interpretations of success. People place different perceptions on what they believe success means. Some people spend their whole life striving for money, quality time, happiness, ways to help others, a respectable job, a better role, a family, heaven, freedom, health, a big house, a nice car, friends, etc. Success, in its fundamental construct, is simple. It is really just getting what you want.

Success is the mental aptitude that one has in order to realize their abilities to get what they want.

The problem is that people don't really know what they want. Of those people who do know *what* they want, many don't know *why* they want it or *how* to get it — or even believe they can have it. In other words, people don't realize their abilities.

There are many abilities that one may have, and many of these provide the capability to achieve other abilities.

Whatever it is that you want to improve your quality of life, you can get it. You can do it. You have *The Abilities*. In other words, this book defines the abilities that will help you get what you want, from desire to legacy.

… Now, let's go get it.

Chapter 1 | Desiring

"The two greatest movers of the human mind are the desire for good, and the fear of evil."
— *Samuel Johnson*

After you read this chapter, close your eyes for a moment and imagine this:

You are lying on your deathbed. While you are lying there, you reflect on your life. You think about all of the things that transpired. The sweet times, the sad times, the shameful times, the happy times. Think about your first kiss, your first job, your best moment. Think about all those memories. For whatever reason, you have kept those memories. But why!? What made it worth it to you? What were you most proud of? What were your struggles? What did you take for granted? What would you do if you had a second chance? What would you change? What gave you fulfillment? What did you live for?

Let me rephrase the point with another question. What do you really, really, really, really,

really, *really* want? *REALLY!* Define it. What drives you? What is your purpose? What makes you, you? What impact do you want to leave? How do you want people to think of you? How do you want to think of yourself? What makes you happy? What do you like to do? What is your passion? What are your fears? How do you want to contribute to society? How do you want to change the world? How can you affect the greatest number of people in the greatest way? Why do you do what you do now?

Defining what you want doesn't just have to be one thing, it can be multiple things. It can be tangible or intangible. It can be big or it can be small. It can be something for you or something for others. You can create and do whatever you choose. The only one that can *help* you and *be* you, and *make* you you, is *you* — and you know that. So again, what is it that *you* want and, more importantly, *why* do you want it?

The first step at getting what you want out of life is to create purposeful goals. I challenge you to write down everything you want, at least fifty things. These goals should be set out using SMARTER approach: S – Specific, M – Measurable, A –

Achievable, R – Relevant, T – Timely, E – Evaluable, R – Revisable.

This is a great practice to help you realize what you want, why you want it and how you will get it. Let's break this down.

Specific: You want your goals to be particular. If your goals are too vague, they are not attainable. Being exact will make it much easier to define how to get there. Think of who, what, why, how, where and which?

Measurable: You cannot control what you do not measure. Think of a way to quantify your progress to attain your goals. Consider how you will know when they are accomplished.

Achievable: If you make your goals too far-fetched, then you can get discouraged. Thinking big is great and is encouraged. However, make stepping stones to your major goals and choose ones that you know you can reach.

Relevant: Make sure your goals are purposeful and you have a reason "why" to each one. Your goals should reflect where and who you want to be once you reach them. Make sure they are worthwhile.

Timely: Set deadlines for your goals and milestones along the way. This will give you a juncture to work toward. Timing is of the essence.

Evaluable: Study your progress to understand the value you have added to your life when striving for your goals. Continually reflect on your goals and assess how you are doing.

Revisable: It is okay to modify your goals as things change. Your life and the world are very dynamic. There are many times when you may change your mind because of lessons learned along the way.

Here are a few examples of some SMARTER goals:

1. I want $2.4MM in revenue generated through my company by the end of this fiscal year. I will accomplish this by twenty new sales monthly with an average of $100K each. I will hire two salesmen to help me reach this goal.

2. I want to quit smoking by the end of July of this year. I will accomplish this by reducing the number of cigarettes I smoke by one each week until I get to zero. Then I will make a vow

to myself to never again allow a cigarette to touch my lips.

3. I want to marry my girlfriend in April of this year. I am going to reserve the location, buy the ring and practice my vows.

4. I want to launch a new energy services company that builds the infrastructure for the future by the end of June of this year. I will start a new entity, build a website, get insurance, sell my first job and recruit four employees, including a field supervisor, a project manager, an administrator and a CPA. I also will retain an attorney.

5. I want to lose twenty-five pounds by the start of the summer. I am going to do two-a-days with thirty minutes of cardio in the morning and lifting in the afternoon with three sets of ten reps. I am going to go on a diet and I will lose two pounds per week.

Once you set your goals, you can develop a precedence of priority for them. You can rank your goals on importance from 1-3, with 1 being most important and 3 being back-burner items. Understand a programmatic approach to getting everything done and coordinate multiple activities at any given time to reach your deadlines.

Exercises & Action Items

1. Close your eyes and think back on your life to determine your purpose.
2. Set SMARTER goals to start driving toward your personal equation of success. Choose your goals wisely.

Implied Abilities

To set goals | To focus on what you want | To realize your purpose | To soul-seek | To find your reason why | To envision

Chapter 2 | Envisioning

"Whether you think you can, or you think you can't, you're right." — *Henry Ford*

Now that you have identified what you want, why you want it and how you are going to get it, it's time to take the next step: *envisioning*. The practice of envisioning is very powerful and there is a lot of power in positive thinking.

Successful people focus on what they want, while unsuccessful people focus on what they don't want. In our current day and age, humans innately have a problem with their lack of attention, leading to a tough time holding onto their goals. It is easy to get sidetracked and lose sight of what you want, especially if it gets hard along the way. It is important to develop a strong enough passion for what you want to retain the ability to see it through.

Close your eyes and envision as if you already have achieved what you want. Think of it as if it is already done. How does having this make you feel? Feelings are a great indicator as to whether you are on the right track. If you feel positive (joyful, excitement, encouragement, love, hopeful, driven, passionate, happiness) that is a good sign. Feelings matter. It is important to tie a strong feeling and passion to your desire. This will help you to remember your reason why and give you endurance along your journey.

Another great technique for remembering and retaining your goals is to create a "vision board". Joining a pictorial depiction in conjunction with your desire acts as a tangible reference you can always look back on. A vision board is a compilation of cutouts from magazines, books, quotes, or printouts related to your desire. When creating a vision board, I challenge you to think of the big picture along with the details. This will make your vision even more powerful.

While money is important, don't focus solely on it, but focus on your purpose as well. Find graphics that show how you are going to change the world and positively impact lives. The money will be a derivative of your purpose. Hang this vision board in your home in a place where you will naturally look at it repeatedly. The more you can remind yourself of your goals, the more likely you are to realize them.

Another way to ensure you hold yourself accountable is to tell people what you are doing. It will not only help you define your vision more clearly through the act of verbal remembrance and iteration, but it also will hold you to having integrity; that is doing what you say you will do.

Cling to what you want, because it won't be easy. You shouldn't want your goals to be easy. If they were easy, everyone would have it and would be doing it. If it were easy, it would not be worth as much to you when you achieve it. This is where holding onto faith and hope becomes a necessary ingredient to your success. I will go further into this later in the chapters titled "Adversity" and "Faith, Hope & Love."

Having an opportunistic mindset through envisioning will help you realize your resources and opportunity at hand. One thought can trigger a series of subsequent thoughts, culminating in a plethora of ideas. Thoughts become things. If your mind is in the right frequency to accept opportunity and you are constantly thinking positive thoughts about what you want, you are more likely to achieve whatever you are thinking about. This plays a huge part in the creative process.

Humans, unlike any other creature, are able to tap into this part of their brain. All other creature's thoughts are instinctual, reactive and critical. Humans, have that as well, but can also tap into this realization of creativity. Creativity is a futuristic comprehension. Envisioning helps you think about what you want. Thinking about what you want helps you focus on the future, and focusing on the future helps you create.

Creating is a beautiful gift. The more you can create, the more you learn. The more you learn, the more you can create. Success is in the eye of the beholder. You cannot attain what you do not see. Think of yourself as an eagle. Eagles have a gift of vision. They have an advantage over other predators because they can see further.

The more you envision yourself as already having achieved what you want and the more you focus on your goals, the more you will attract the resources and opportunities that you need to be successful.

Exercises & Action Items

1. Close your eyes and envision as if you already have attained what you want.
2. Create a vision board.
3. Practice thinking positive thoughts and exercise your faith and hope.
4. Pray and meditate often; say thanks and ask for what you want.

Implied Abilities

To develop a passion | To see it through | To gain endurance | To remind | To cling on to what you want | To create | To have a positive mindset | To change

Chapter 3 | Changing

"We cannot solve our problems with the same thinking we used when we created them."
— *Albert Einstein*

It's a bit overwhelming going into your new-found desire with all the unknowns and change, and thinking about who you are going to be, and what you are going to do. Fear of the unknown is a common reality. Take a deep breath! You're going to be okay! Just hold on to your passion and take that truth into your journey. There is never a wrong journey, only a journey that is never taken. And God will take care of you. No journey is wrong, so take the journey.

The majority of people try to avoid change because it makes them feel uncomfortable. People become stagnant through all the knowns, rituals and similarities. While it is good to find what rings true to your heart and what you like, I challenge you to get out of your box as well. Build on top of the things that you hold onto and experience the blessing of newness.

You need to believe in yourself. Believe that you can do it and believe that you deserve it. Your dreams can come true if you have the courage to pursue them. Let your choices be driven by your hopes, not your fears.

Overcoming your fear of change offers many blessings, the greatest of which is learning. You should try to learn something new every day. The only thing constant in this world is change. If you embrace that, you will come to realize that dynamics are healthy and a necessary ingredient of success.

Change requires work, there is no doubt about it. You must force yourself to get out of your comfort zone and put in the effort. It is inevitable. Laziness is detrimental to your success and procrastination will impede your ability to achieve what you want.

Don't be afraid to ask questions and do research. You don't know what you don't know, plus, the more you know the better off you are. Everyone must start somewhere, even if that means commencing in naivety. Understand your boundaries and where you can break down the walls. Sometimes the smallest of changes can achieve the largest of results.

Not only does this world offer a wealth of information that will be necessary on your journey of changing, but today's seasons will change as well. You need to learn to ebb and flow with the current circumstances and apply different solutions to the existing environment. Different people and situations require unique approaches. Switching up your technique to derive a different result can be revolutionary.

Learn to compartmentalize what works and what doesn't work. Take everything with a grain of salt. Try to retain as much information as you can. You never know when you might need that record and how you may use that information to your advantage in the future. Learn from your past, live in the present and change the future.

This is the most admirable trait that one can have: ability to adapt. It makes one wise, creative, willing to learn and, most importantly, diverse.

Exercises & Action Items

1. Challenge yourself.
2. Put in the work to learn something new every day.
3. Embrace change.

Implied Abilities

To take the journey | To start somewhere | To learn | To overcome fear | To be new | To adapt | To grow

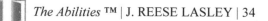

Chapter 4 | Growing

"Change is inevitable, but progress is optional."
— *Tony Robbins*

Take growth extremely seriously. If you are not growing, you're dying. When you grow, you live. Life grows. Growth is imperative.

There are many situations you can put yourself in that may cause change, yet not growth. You always want to progress. You always want to be a better you — always.

There are various forms of growth. The most obvious and easiest answer is to grow financially. Most people are consumed by money. Whether they like it or not, money runs their lives. Money is a great tool and we all can use more money. It is the basis of trade and working together. However, sometimes the experience is worth more than the money. Sometimes, in fact, money can be a hindrance to growth, or be destructive to it.

You can grow in friendships, family, health, love, happiness, lessons learned, best practices and in many other ways. In other words, all your goals you set forth in Chapter One can and should grow.

Take a seed, for example. Imagine this seed is your goal. You can plant your seed, but there are many variables to determining just how it will burst into life and the quality of life that it can potentially have. Where you plant it will determine how it will grow. If it is planted on rocky ground, too close to weeds or in a desert, it may not have the opportunity to grow. Also, the means you take after your seed is planted will determine how it will grow. Growth requires constant nurturing. If you make something else a priority, your seed will not flourish. The goal is for your seed to bloom and be lush. "We reap the same in kind that we sow" *Matthew* 13 — KJV Bible.

Are you actually able to give your goal what it needs to thrive? Can you figure out what you need to get what you want? Are you in the right circumstances to grow? Do you need to change anything? What do you need to make your success most probable?

Look at everything as an opportunity to grow. Everything in life is like a battery. It is all about how you look at things. Things can be positive or negative. Your mindset has the potential to derive what you are looking for. Success is in the eye of the beholder. Don't turn away from something because you don't like it or don't like doing it. Sometimes that is exactly what you need to grow.

Many people place judgments on this world before they truly understand the things they are judging. Always keep an open mind and don't turn away from anything unless you have done your research. Furthermore, even if you have learned to turn away from something because it hurt you or didn't help you in the past, it may be worth investigating again. Ask yourself: Can this help me grow? How have I grown in the process? What is it worth to me?

Don't get discouraged by the negators in life. Don't let people or obstacles ever hold you back. Never let other people steal your dreams. Don't listen to the noes – listen to the yeses. It is simply by virtue of trying that determines your growth.

I have been through many successes and also many disappointments in my life, but I never let the disappointments stop me. Success comes in cans, not in cannots. There have been many amazing people in history who have heard many noes and failed many times, but it was the yes inside of them that made them successful, and even famous. Yeses are far stronger than all of the noes that can ever be offered.

A significant element to growth is time. Allow yourself the time to grow. Things can change and grow at different paces. Various elements require less or more frequent approaches, especially when you're working together. Managing multiple goals and resources at one time can be very complex and slow your growth. Multitasking can be very constructive or destructive. If your growth is not happening as quickly as you would like, ask yourself, Why? Try to determine the root of the issue. Refer to your precedence of priority and reassess your timeline.

You can do everything in your power to create change and grow, but sometimes you need to accept what you cannot change. Let your goals take on a life of their own and support them along the way. If you are not getting the results you would like to see, try switching up your strategy because sometimes what you firmly believe may actually delay your desired manifestation.

Sometimes by realizing you are not in control creates the growth you are looking for. Think about your end goal and be creative with how you can get there. Sometimes it may not look exactly like you expected, but focus on what really matters. Analyze the state of affairs to determine if you are headed in the right direction. Ask yourself if you are being distracted by the things that are not of God – and how you can reach your full potential that He has in store for you. Remain faithful, focused, persistent and keep striving. Measure your progress and don't be afraid to test and modify.

You also need to make sure you can sustain your growth. There is risk involved with growing. The worst thing that can happen is for you to attempt to grow too fast, not be able to sustain it and not be able to recover. So take calculated risk and manage your progress and resources.

The intention is that you may fill your life with a variety of fruits, flowers and blessings. Understand when you need to provide nutrients, sun and water to your goals to endure the seasons to come.

Exercises & Action Items

1. Don't settle for loss.
2. Measure your growth and your goals.
3. If things aren't going to plan, find the root of the issue, test and modify.
4. Change your strategy if needed.

Implied Abilities

To live | To experience | To build | To thrive | To chase your dreams | To find | To sustain | To measure | To manifest | To create | To manage risk

Chapter 5 | Risk Management

"There can be no great accomplishment without risk."

— *Neil Armstrong*

Everything that you do has risk involved. Whether you are driving to work, falling in love or starting a new business, you will be bombarded with threats along the way. You may have heard the common "risk vs. reward" statement. That is very true. You will never get to where you want to go without taking risk. It is just part of the game. The question is, How much risk are you able and willing to take, and can you manage it?

Your level of audacity is a personal choice, which has the potential to affect other people. Risk, just like success, is relative. Understand what you're dealing with.

You need to be smart about what makes something worth it to you and what makes it worth it to others. Everyone is in a different place in life. If you are eighty-five years old, you may be more reluctant to drive your car due to poor eyesight. If you are forty years old with a family, you may not be able to risk all of your money on starting a new venture, because their lives depend on it. If you are falling in love, you are risking that the other person will treat you the way you should be treated and vice versa.

Understand where your portfolio of risk lies, and what you can and cannot do. Analyze where you currently are in your life and where you want to go – and then determine if it is worth it. This is the responsible way of going about anything you want. You do not want to hurt yourself or others if you can avoid it. Choose the right opportunity wisely per the risk associated with it by carefully weighing your opportunity costs. This is governed by the basic law of cause and effect. Everything you do is a conditional formula that impacts something or someone else.

Where it is commendable to be a positive person and always seek out opportunity, it is just as important to manage that opportunity. Playing the devil's advocate by running scenarios of probability and impact if risks do occur, will help you make intelligent choices. This exercise can save you a lot of time, money and issues. It has the potential to save you from falling short of success.

Prepare a document that breaks down the activities of your goals. Spreadsheets are good for this. The activities could be financials, materials, time, unforeseen conditions, possible experiences, personnel, equipment, legal, etc. Then, create two columns ranking 1-10; 1 being the least and 10 being the most. One column should be titled "Probability", the other column should be titled "Impact". Rank all of your activities on this scale. This will give you a quadrant of scenarios.

1. Low probability and low impact.
2. Low probability and high impact.
3. High probability and low impact.
4. High probability and high impact.

Once you have identified the activities by their level of probability and impact, create another column for "Mitigations". Start with the activities of highest probability and highest impact first, then move down the list. Come up with three to five potential ways that you can mitigate these risks if and when they occur, and then address what your plan is to remedy them.

Risk management is just like playing a game of chess. You think about all of your pieces on the board. Each one of these pieces can move in different ways and can affect your upcoming moves. You should always think at least five steps ahead of where you are going. This requires brainpower and a complex approach to decision making. Just as in chess, you have to be careful with where you move, consider your opponent (or risk) from all angles, make your decision and then make your move.

This forces you to think about yourself and your surroundings. This makes you run scenarios in your head in order to arrive at the best possible outcome.

Success is not easy. There is no exact path to success. It can be achieved in multiple different ways. The more you practice, though, the better you get at overcoming obstacles. Keep in mind that if you never try, you will never experience success.

It is a clever idea to find a network of like-minded individuals who have been through what you are going through. These people can be advisors, mentors, friends or just anyone that cares about your success. Make sure you choose your network carefully because these people will be significant in providing their interpretation of the chess board. Always keep in mind that you are the one taking the risk, not them. Whereas the input and assistance are appreciated, you may understand your position better than they ever will. You are the one ultimately making the decision. Don't just do something because someone else tells you to. Think about it. Hard. Then act in your (and other's) best interest.

In your process of growing and changing on your journey through envisioning your goals, take a calculated approach to risk vs. reward. This will make things easier for you and others.

Exercises & Action Items
1. Create a risk management plan.
2. If appropriate, ask others for input.

Implied Abilities

To risk | To chase | To weigh opportunity costs | To determine worth | To be smart | To measure | To find | To sustain | To think | To make a decision | To understand probability and impact | To choose | To take action

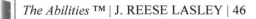

Chapter 6 | Action

"Knowledge is not power. The application of knowledge is power." — *Daryl Turner*

We live in the information age. Every day we are given new data, new technology and new understanding. We are so blessed to live in this era. We have all the information we want and need at our fingerprints. Never before in history has this been possible. The efficiencies and productivities that this affords us are incredible. We are very lucky and should not take this for granted.

In 1597 Sir Francis Bacon claimed that "knowledge itself is power." However, where knowledge is the foundation of power, knowledge without action is useless. We have to take this information, create data, make decisions and then execute.

Learn to work smart and hard. Strategy, used in conjunction with action, will create results. You have a choice either do something, or nothing. You can act in innumerable ways that will serve your purpose. The trick is finding the simplest approach to getting the results you want. Growth creates experience, experience begets wisdom, wisdom produces simplicity. Genius is your ability to do things right the first time. If you can act with the right information, in the right way, at the right time, you can create miraculous manifestations. That will make you a genius.

There is a fine balance between wanting and getting. Many people want something, but few are willing to get it. Many people struggle with trying to be perfect before they deploy, or let fear of risk halt their progress. What many folks fail to recognize is that perfection is a journey. It's about the journey, so go ahead and take the journey. Remember, you miss 100% of the shots you never take. And perfection, much like success, is in the eye of the beholder.

Try not to have paralysis by analysis. If you overthink things, you will never get what you want. At some point, you will have to make a decision — and go! What you will find is that a lot of the hardship of analyzing how you will figure things out will disappear when you are figuring things out.

Make daily lists with precedence of priority. You have your goals, you understand your risk, you are learning and growing in the process, now all you need to do is organize your thoughts and work on them every day. You can make a calendar, or a schedule or an hourly breakdown of activities in your day. However you want to do it, just make sure you cross off your accomplishments — and always be creating more.

It also is important to recognize your talent, your strengths and your weaknesses, as well as others'. You don't have to know everything or do everything. A large part of success is delegation. Understand what you can do to get others to work with and for you. The best way to do this is find what they want that shares your common purpose. Communicate effectively and create deliverable goals with a schedule.

Keep in mind, that no matter how good you and your team are at doing something, there is always the element of luck. It is better to be lucky than good, and the harder (and smarter) you work, the more luck you will find. Most of the time you grind and a little of the time you shine. Keep at it for a long enough period of time, though, and eventually you will be blessed with a stroke of luck.

Exercises & Action Items

1. You have your eagle vision. Now spread your wings. Fly! Experience what this amazing life has to offer.
2. Create your daily action items list and prioritize.
3. Do!

Implied Abilities

To do | To experience | To work | To have a mission | To create results | To manifest | To apply | To list | To fly | To determine precedence of priority | To earn

Chapter 7 | Earning

"There are three ingredients in the good life: learning, earning and yearning." — *Christopher Morley*

While it is a blessing to have someone there to help you along the way, or to receive an inheritance or to win the lottery, there is something to be said about the person who started from nothing or the one who didn't just take the prize offered up on a silver platter, even though they could. You want to be the one who didn't just take the easiest way. The person who actually earned their keep, and made it happen. The person who put in the work and faced the adversity. The one who stood up to the challenge, and got the A in life. That is the person who *earned* it, and really understands what it is worth. Who do you know in your life that lives up to that honor?

We all know those other people. The kids who ruin everything because they don't understand the value of it. The teenagers who get addicted to drugs because they have no purposeful goals to work toward. The people that are so wealthy that they don't appreciate what they have because it can be so easily replaced. The person that continually lies to you because they can, even though you know they are taking advantage of you. The common denominator with all of these examples is that these people are inconsiderate and indifferent.

I find that the people who never earn anything are ungrateful and even disrespectful. They have all of the luxuries of having what they want without knowing what it took to get it. They don't even know how to be mindful to others' needs because they don't understand how hard other people worked for it or how much it means to them. They don't honor what they are given. The people who never earn anything take everything for granted.

Some people need a reality check that everything and everyone around us has value. The amount of work that had to go into getting your paint on the wall, or pay for your dinner date or put shoes on your feet, took effort. The person who makes you coffee in morning at the local café — that person has a story. They matter. They are on their own journey of life, of discovery, of earning their way. We should be grateful for them and, therefore, considerate of others.

The majority of the world has barely anything. The ironic thing is that those are some of the most giving, humble and hardworking people. Our American society, in general, has it very cushy and, as a result, we tend to not take the time to appreciate the little things in life. Most people don't put much thought into understanding what it took to get what they bought from the grocery store — or realize the conveniences of modern day life in general.

People place different degrees on what is and what is not valuable to them. Some people place a lower degree of valuation on things and some people place a higher degree of valuation on things. Where something may not mean a lot to you, it may mean the world to another. Value is relative. One man's trash is another man's treasure.

Realize that when you do get what you want, it doesn't make you better than anyone else. Yes, you earned it and you should have a selfless pride, but that doesn't give you the right to boast. The only way you should be looking down on someone is by helping them up.

The key here is appreciation and gratitude. Earning something produces self-respect. If someone gives you a gift, honor it. If someone produces a service, appreciate it. Don't take things for granted. Work hard, be humble, honor the people and things around you.

Exercises & Action Items

1. Earn what you want.
2. Realize and appreciate what people and things are worth.
3. Be humble.

Implied Abilities

To understand worth | To honor | To appreciate | To understand why | To get to the next level | To be considerate | To be grateful | To be humble | To face adversity

Chapter 8 | Adversity

"Great men rejoice in adversity, just as brave soldiers triumph in war." — *Seneca*

It is not the obstacle, or trial, or tribulation, or hardship, or setback, or challenge that determines your character. It's how you handle it — and move forward — that determines your character.

It's not always easy. No matter who you are, where you go or what you do, you will be faced with adversity at some juncture. You are only as good as the amount of adversity that you can handle.

There are three different philosophies on conflict:

1. Avoidance: Some people avoid conflict at all expense. Conflict makes them uncomfortable. They can't handle the negativity or they overreact to the world when it is unfair.

2. Inevitableness: Some people understand conflict is inevitable. They deal with conflict as it comes and face their problems head on.

3. Perpetration: Some people create conflict. These people believe conflict creates change so they induce duress into their own and other's lives.

I believe there is a place and time for all three of these scenarios. When I look back on the conflict in my life, I find that those are the times when I experienced the most growth. Hindsight is 20/20. These are the times where my feet were put to the fire, where my bravery was tested and where I became a better me. So, "bring on the rain."

If you can learn and/or help others learn the easy way, that is obviously preferred. However, sometimes it takes hitting rock bottom to create necessary transformation. Sometimes it just takes that little bit of pain to help you realize your full potential — and that you need to change.

Of the most admirable traits that anyone can have is the ability to overcome. Overcoming your fears, overcoming your pain, overcoming your weaknesses, overcoming your shortcomings. These make you stronger.

If you have never seen the movie *Rocky*, I recommend you watch it. There is a brilliant scene where Rocky is talking to his son. He goes on to tell his son one of the greatest declarations of all time. He proclaims, "Let me tell you something you already know. The world ain't all sunshine and rainbows. It's a very mean and nasty place, and I don't care how tough you are, it will beat you to your knees and keep you there permanently if you let it. You, me or nobody is gonna hit as hard as life. But it ain't about how hard you hit. It's about how hard you can get hit and keep moving forward; how much you can take and keep moving forward. That's how winning is done! Now, if you know what you're worth, then go out and get what you're worth. But you gotta be willing to take the hits and not pointing fingers saying you ain't where you wanna be because of him, or her or anybody. Cowards do that and that ain't you. You're better than that!"

Rocky is an inspiration and a man of integrity. He is a fighter. This scene draws an analogy between boxing and facing adversity boldly. Where I am not encouraging you to run around the streets hitting people for no reason, you need to know when to defend yourself. You need to be prepared to retaliate. Life is not fair. People and situations will take advantage of you. You need to be able to recognize when you are walking through the valley of the shadow of death — and figure a way to get out of it.

Sin can beget sin. Sin also can paradoxically create blessings if people can overcome the sin. Fighting fire with fire may not always be the best solution. It is very easy to get caught up in a downward spiral of sin and negativity. Sometimes the hardest thing to do is to let go of your pride, turn the other cheek and choose to be positive.

There is a huge difference between constructive behavior and destructive behavior. Think about how you are going to react to get what you want, and do it in a way that best accommodates your

purpose. Sometimes when others go low, you need to go high.

You need to be able to protect yourself and do your best to protect others as well. Treat people as you wish to be treated. This is the Golden Rule. If everyone could stick to that, the world would be a better place. However, people are different, people don't always have a common purpose and people have different timelines. Working together can be a blessing and a curse. That is where ethics comes into play. This is why attorneys make so much money. Perceptions and beliefs are subjective, and facts and truth are objective. Realize which you are dealing with.

The worst disease known to mankind is "excusitus." Excusitus is where someone places blame on anything and everything, and anyone and everyone else, instead of accepting fault and figuring out how they can grow from it. Internalizing the issue and figuring out what you can do to make the situation better to personally improve is always the better route.

Justifying your stance, helping others understand the sequence of events, realizing the truth, or holding firm in your beliefs is completely acceptable. These can be strong retaliation tactics. However, don't settle for a loss, and always look internally to find how you can improve, help others, make things good and get what you want.

Build up endurance. You don't need to solve all your problems at once, you just need to continue solving them to live and fight the battle another day. An over accumulation of stress can hurt you. Learn to deal with the adversity — be relentless, remain strong and hold onto your faith.

Exercises & Action Items
1. Keep your head up and keep going.
2. Avoid "excusitus."

Implied Abilities
To prepare | To handle conflict | To fight | To protect | To become stronger | To figure it out | To know worth | To retaliate | To solve | To build endurance | To overcome | To find integrity

Chapter 9 | Integrity

"Trust has two dimensions: competence and integrity. We will forgive mistakes of competence. Mistakes of integrity are harder to overcome." — *Simon Sinek*

Integrity is doing what you say you will do, and doing what is right, even if that means sacrifice. The point of having integrity is building trust. Trust is a must. You must live in the truth — every day.

In the last chapter, I discussed the worst disease known to mankind, which is "excusitus." The people who find every excuse in the world for their failure will never grow. They hurt others, can't be trusted and are unreliable. Don't succumb to the level of these people. Always be a person of your word and of your purpose, even if others let you down.

Lack of integrity can be detrimental to your reputation. Your good name is everything. Lack of integrity also can make you doubt yourself. If you do what you know is wrong, then you will become upset with yourself and start to believe lies. You need to look within and find your peace with the situation, even if it isn't the easiest thing to do. Follow what is good. You know what is right in your heart of hearts.

People live in secrets. They hide from the truth because of many reasons. Some people don't want to accept their downfall and live in denial. Some people can't accept the cost. Some people actually have good intentions and want to protect others. Some people are cruel and want to take advantage of you. Some people live selfishly or are addicted to certain behaviors, knowing others don't accept their actions. This is common and is something you should recognize about the human race. All have fallen short of the glory.

There is sacrifice and risk associated with doing the right thing. Sometimes you have to give away what you want for the greater good. Sometimes there is an expense with doing the right thing, whether that means money, or pride, or relationships, or trust. You can only hope that the people you work with have as much integrity as you. Naïve mistakes are much easier to forgive than ones of repetition, time and knowingness. Dragging something on can drag you and others down. Try to nip issues in the bud before they have the opportunity to become detrimental.

The ironic thing is that most people can accept the cold hard truth, but cannot accept the long drawn out lie. Most of the time you will grow your trust with another person if things are brought into the light in the beginning. Most people will find a way to work with or through them.

Beware of the person who lies to cover their lies, to cover more lies. Their lives are ticking bombs. It is only a matter of time before they get what they gave.

You should always under promise and over deliver. Don't count your chickens before they hatch and don't put other people in the predicament of trying to figure out if the chicken or the egg will come first. There are some things you just cannot control. If something that is out of your control affects another person negatively, be honorable, communicate and figure out a way to correct the issue. Make a plan to remedy the matter.

To make yourself better at the expense of others is flawed thinking. The people who do this end up actually causing more loss between all parties than they would gain if they just helped others. I will go more into this in the chapter titled "Win-Win".

Setting realistic expectations for your goals is so important. You don't want to reach a point where you or others are let down. But if you do reach that point, you want to be able to figure out how to get to what is right and where you want to go.

You see, success is not success at all if you don't feel good about it when you get there. Success without integrity is failure. If you had to sacrifice your best friend for money, have you really gained that much? If you had to steal from multiple people to help other people, does that make you a good person? If you took juice to become huge and then had a heart attack, did you win?

Keep your eye on the prize and what really matters. Failure is giving up on yourself and what you really want. When you look back on your life, if you didn't get to where you wanted to go in an honorable way, it won't have been worth it.

Exercises & Action Items

1. Do what you say you are going to do.
2. Stuff happens. Deal with it in the right, pure, honorable and good way.
3. Don't use excuses.
4. Live in the truth.

Implied Abilities

To do the right thing | To trust | To sacrifice | To live up to your word | To uphold reputation | To under promise and over deliver | To take ownership | To set realistic expectations | To manage resources

Chapter 10 | Resources

"Fools ignore complexity. Pragmatists suffer it. Some can avoid it. Geniuses remove it." — *Alan Perils*

Managing your resources is a large part of upholding integrity. You have to do everything in your power to control what you can and manage others' expectations. Sometimes that requires a lot of coordination, communication and creativity.

Resources include money, time, people, material, equipment — anything that it takes to get the job done. Think about what you have at your disposal. Then try to figure out what the most efficient and productive way is to get that to work with and/or for you. There are a million different ways to leverage your resources and a million different ways to get to your end result. There is no one formula or clear-cut way to success. Sometimes it is just that minor change or one unique thing you have at your disposal that makes all the difference. Sometimes it's an array of resources that work together.

Resources can *be* very complex or very simple. Resources can *make* things very complex or *make* things very simple.

Your mental aptitude is your greatest asset when it comes to realizing what is available to you and how to deal with resources. This can be a natural talent or a skill you have learned. Being able to realize what someone or something else could bring to the table could give you what you need. Sometimes leveraging one resource will enable you to capitalize on another. You may not always have all the answers, but someone else very well might.

Your introverted and extroverted selves will be put to the test here. Realize that your success depends on your ability to manage your own actions, as well as the actions of your resources. Investigate what your capabilities are and what each resource may or may not be able to do. There are many things within (and also outside of) your control. Sometimes you must accept what you cannot control and reassess your resource strategy.

Where you need to be able to solve problems, you also need to be able to ask the right questions. William Shakespeare wrote, "A fool thinks himself to be wise, but a wise man knows himself to be a fool." You will find yourself asking a lot of questions. For example: How much money do I have to invest? Who knows what do in this situation? Do I need a subject matter expert right now? What tools do I need? What can those tools do? How much time do I have? What are some other options? How could I save time and money? Is there a better way?

Resources are the basis of your competitive edge. They are what makes you different — and what makes you unique.

Exercises & Action Items

1. Be creative in realizing what resources are at your disposal and discover the best way to utilize them.

2. When you find what works, stick with it, but always build, always innovate and always improve.

Implied Abilities

To control | To accept what you cannot control | To coordinate | To get the job done | To think creatively | To realize external and internal abilities | To manage | To use | To communicate | To be competitive | To diversify

Chapter 11 | Diversification

"You must be diversified enough to survive tough times or bad luck so that skill and good process can have the chance to pay off over the long term."
— *Joon Greenblatt*

Diversification is key. It is the best risk mitigation. The more you can diversify your portfolio — in whatever arena — the more secure you will be.

Insecurity is the fastest route to failure. It is always good to hedge your bet. Everything has the potential to fail for one reason or another. If one thing fails, always make sure you have a backup plan, if not ten. Whether it is stocks, or resources, or playbooks or businesses, the more you do the more probable you are to find success.

Diversification allows you to play with high and low risk at the same time. If you can test the waters on multiple fronts, you can equalize the losses and success of multiple efforts at once. The more you do something, the more an average starts to appear. Therefore, if you are able to consistently measure an assortment of like and unalike initiatives, the more protected you will be while figuring out what works.

Diversification is a good sign of success. Diversification insinuates intelligence, wisdom and experience. A multifaceted approach to success gives you more opportunity.

Diversification also can be a burden. If you diversify too quickly you may not have the resources to uphold integrity. If you diversify too much in the same arena you could dilute your niche. You have to know what you are doing before you diversify. You need to learn and practice before you jump in. Find avenues to research, to investigate or to fail at without consequence first.

Exercises & Action Items
1. Diversify intelligently.
2. Hedge your bets.
3. Have multiple backup plans.

Implied Abilities

To mitigate risk | To hedge | To multiply | To be different | To win

Chapter 12 | Win-Win

"Every man must decide whether he will walk in the
light of creative altruism or in the darkness of
destructive selfishness." — *Martin Luther King Jr.*

Finding people in your life who think and care
about others' well-being, as well as their own, is rare.
The majority of people think mostly of themselves and
their own interest. This is a hard reality. Most people
will take advantage of you to get further in life
(whether they are aware of it or not) — that's just the
way it is.

If there is a way to help others succeed while you
succeed, take it. You should be just as enthusiastic
about the success of others as you are about your
own.

One horse can pull one thousand pounds, but two
horses together can pull four thousand pounds. Why
is that? It is because there is a lot of value in the
space between. Working together with people is one

of the most rewarding things to be able to do. It pushes you and makes you better. It is also one of the hardest skillsets to learn and to put into practice. However, the leverage you gain through soft skills and being able to work with others will get you way further in life than by always doing everything on your own.

Be the bigger person. Create a positive reputation by caring about others' well-being. I promise you, you will win in a greater way because of this.

There are four scenarios which make up the quadrant of winning and losing:

1. Win-Win
2. Win-Lose
3. Lose-Win
4. Lose-Lose

Creating win-win is the best situation, and taking a loss for a greater purpose is better than taking a win for yourself while hurting someone else. Over time, you will gain way more through doing this than by taking advantage of others. The only time I would advise to take a win while someone else has a loss, is when the loss is *temporary* and you know you will make a win for both parties in due time. Figure out ways you can stay in the win-win quadrant and never create a loss to any party.

Building relationships is an important ability in attaining success. You always want to build constructive relationships and steer away from the destructive ones. You don't necessarily need to be the smartest or the best at everything. Understand your personal strengths and weaknesses, and where others can use their strengths to benefit you. It is not only what you know, but also who you know.

This requires an ability to give and to take. You should provide a foot up to others any chance you can. It also should be that way for all other parties involved. Everyone should be offering a foot up to others instead of always having a hand out. Beware of leeches and people that use you, but never give anything back. It is much more blessed to give than to receive. This does not mean you always have to be the one giving, but it means that (going back to the horse analogy) everyone should be pulling their weight.

The people who take advantage of others promote a losing proposition and ultimately make everyone, including themselves, lose. They inevitably attract their karma in due time. We lose respect and trust for people like this, and those people only end up hurting both themselves and others.

Fairness: You must figure out what is fair. Fairness is very subjective. What makes it worth it to you may not be what makes it worth it to someone else. And figuring out what makes it worth it to someone else is not always easy. Some people have less and some people have more. If you are going between one spectrum to the other, there needs to be some sort of promise, medium of trade, agreement, understanding or an expression of giving.

We live in a capitalistic environment and we are naturally competitive, but we should try to make cooperative moves as well. I call this "co-opetition." This really comes down to professional negotiations, understanding of other's needs, making intelligent decisions and ethics.

People do not want to be taken advantage of, period. If someone breaks an agreement, trust is lost — and trust means everything. If you cannot trust someone you cannot work together. This goes for all levels of relationships, both personal and professional. If something happens that is not right then you must make it right. Else, you will suffer in your social health and your good name will be tarnished overtime. You want to be known and remembered as the person who always cared and as someone of integrity.

Greed: Greed is a sure way to lose honor in business and personal life. Nobody likes the people who are only out for themselves. Nobody wants to work with these people over the long-term. Those who consistently think of only their benefit and not of others, will become known as the takers. Nobody wants to help these people. Greed will separate you from your full potential and hinder your ability to succeed.

There is a lot of wisdom that derives from helping others. They say the best way to learn is to teach. The reason for this is because if you teach, you put yourself into the perspective of another. This helps you think like others and their motives by internalizing their consciousness. If you stay stuck in your own mental realm you will never be able to fully understand or reach others. You may not agree with everything they do and think about, but at least you have empathy and sympathy, enabling you to make rational decisions for the greater good.

Exercises & Action Items

1. Be the bigger person and always do what is right.
2. Help others succeed every chance you get.

Implied Abilities

To care | To unite | To work with | To leverage | To build relationships | To use strengths | To understand relativity | To help others get what they want in conjunction with what you want | To teach | To lead

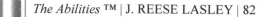

Chapter 13 | Leadership

"Leadership is the art of getting someone else to do
something you want done because they want to do it."
— *Dwight D. Eisenhower*

Who is it in your life that has always been there to
make you better? Who can you think of that always
brings value to you? Think about the traits of these
people and why these people are so auspicious. They
give. They are mindful. They are thoughtful to others
and aware of their environment and situations. These
traits come with the territory of being a leader, of
being able to contribute to other's lives in a positive
way.

Nobody does something for nothing. Everyone has
a purpose, a want, a need or a goal. If you can find
what people want, and help them get it, it is the best
way to leverage their success unto yours. Don't just
assume you know what other people want.
Investigate their desires and figure out a creative way

to assist in their success, while supporting your own objectives. This is definitely a win-win.

Leaders emerge through natural selection, drive, experience, politics and serving others. The people who have learned the ability to help others and make win-win situations are those that naturally rise to the top.

There is a significant difference between leadership and management. Management comes with the power to oversee multiple people and their roles in order to get a job done. Leaders, however, go beyond that. They inspire others to make themselves and their organization grow. Good leaders understand that people are their greatest asset and they will nurture those people like a garden.

The ability to lead will give you the leverage to elevate your own desires and objectives. Think of this as an equal scale or a children's teeter-totter in a playground. If you want to be equal to one million dollars, for example, you will need to get other people on your team to help you gain leverage.

I can explain this best with the parable of the pinecone: There are two gentlemen who are looking for work, Joe and Bob. They both speak to a rancher named Fletcher who has too many pinecones on his land and wants to remove them. Fletcher tells both of them that he would pay $1 per bag of pinecones collected. Both agree and commence work.

Joe works all day. His productivity is one bag of pinecones per hour, making his eight-hour day worth $8. Bob, on the other hand, knows how to be a leader and leverage the situation. He recognizes that the ranch has a lot of opportunity to make money due to the excessive number of pinecones. So Bob goes out and hires eight people who work for .50¢ per bag of pinecones collected. All of the workers are very happy to work for that and Bob justifies their salary based on their desire, his own risk, expenses and providing the opportunity.

They all have the same productivity of one bag per hour. At the end of the day each one of the eight workers walks away with $4 in their pocket. Bob walks away with $40 — $8 of his own labor and $32 from all his eight workers. In summary, Bob makes ten times as much as his employees and five times as much as Joe because he has the ability to lead.

This parable works with all types of reward, not just money, but you get the point. Of course, real life situations are much more complex than this. Ultimately, if you can get others to work with and for you, you will tap into larger growth potential.

The ability to help others help you (and vice versa) is a virtue. Remember, this is the Golden Rule: Treat others as you want to be treated. Kindness, gratitude and humility are just as important as intelligence, technical experience and drive. Your EQ (emotional quotient) needs to be just as savvy as your IQ (intellectual quotient); soft and hard skills are both equally important. These are the key elements to bridging the gap between working with others and being a leader.

Always lead by example. You are only as good as the people that follow you. Put yourself on the front line and always do what you expect of others. Don't be a hypocrite or others will lose your tracks. You need to know how to think quickly and how to make decisions.

Leaders use all the traits mentioned in the prior chapters. They know what they want. They have a vision for how to get it. They undergo rapid change and growth. They take calculated risk. They act on behalf of themselves, others and their organization. They earn their titles. They face more adversity than the average person. They uphold integrity, especially because so many people depend on them. They manage multiple resources. They diversify their portfolios and have sophisticated minds — and finally, they help others constantly.

Exercises & Action Items

1. Put all the action items from previous chapters into practice.
2. Find a way to teach others.
3. Investigate others' desires and don't assume you know what other people want.
4. Think of creative ways to help people get what they want, while supporting your own objectives.

Implied Abilities

To add value to others | To help others help you | To attain an EQ and an IQ | To leverage | To be an example | To give | To be mindful | To follow | To help | To be wise | To nurture | To lead | To understand ethics

Chapter 14 | Ethics

"Moral philosophy is nothing else but the science of what is good, and evil, in the conversation, and society of mankind. Good, and evil, are names that signify our appetites, and aversions; which in different tempers, customs, and doctrines of men, are different." — *Thomas Hobbes*

Everyone is different, everyone has unalike needs and everyone has their own intentions. Ethics come into play when directives, actions, beliefs or desires are not aligned with multiple parties. They also become apparent when there are multiple choices that one may have while weighing out opportunity costs or being pulled in multiple directions. Sometimes it is hard to align the stars when you have different perspectives on the universe.

Sometimes current circumstances lead to being unable to create ideal outcomes. While working together with other people, stakeholders and organizations, there may come a time when you find that you cannot serve all simultaneously. Sometimes you have to choose to act on behalf of one party or another. Sometimes you have to pick the lesser of several evils and yours or others' idyllic model of "right" cannot be fulfilled due to less than ideal conditions and synergies.

The goal, obviously, is to always do what is good and positively contribute to others, but if you can't, try and be creative to find solutions where you can. Most of the time, if you put in a little more research or talk to enough people with the right experience, you will find ways to act in good faith and make ethical decisions.

Live in the truth. I cannot stress this enough. Many people get stuck between a rock and a hard place and feel like they need to lie to get out of it. Sometimes it works, but it is very risky. When you live in deceit, you risk relationships and trust.

People have a hard time being humble, letting go of their pride and bringing their less than ideal situations or mistakes to the light. People sometimes choose to live in the dark, especially if a situation could inflict pain on another party. What's ironic is that the reason people lie is because they don't want to hurt others or themselves, but they fail to recognize that the deceit is actually worse than the inequity. People can respect and work with someone who is willing to admit the cold hard truth and work toward improvement. On the contrary, people have a much harder time giving mercy to the person who lives in the long, drawn out falsity of sin.

Sin derives sin — and it quickly compounds negativity. It is a ticking bomb and the longer the sin compounds, the more exponential the blast. This downward spiral has the ability to impale your livelihood. Don't get caught in this turbulence. If you are in it, get out as fast as you can. This is where the devil thrives and attacks. His forte is understanding your weaknesses and making you believe lies.

Everyone tells lies and all have fallen short of the glory of truth at some point in their life. Acknowledging this fact will help you understand how to work within the confines of good and evil. Be careful whom you choose to listen to. God gave you a choice. You have your own free will to make all the decisions in your life, so choose wisely.

There are a lot of great people in this world, but there are not very many truly good people. Ethics is the fine line between good and great. In this case, "good" takes the mantle of purity. What I mean by this, is that many people get what they want, but didn't do the right thing to get it. If you do not feel good about your success when you attain it, then it's not worth it. Strive to be good — and great. Do the right thing to achieve greatness.

Be a spirit of virtue. Virtue is defined as "behavior showing high moral standards." While you walk through the valley of the shadow of death, develop your character through defending your stance on what you believe is right. If you don't stand for something, you'll stand for anything.

Learn the difference between what's objective and what's subjective. This is critical. Objective means facts. It is something that cannot be disproven. It is a hard-set certainty. Subjective means belief. This is something that is arguable, something based upon feelings or opinions.

This world is not always black and white and many times people's decisions exist in the shades of grey. People bend rules, they can alter their beliefs, and they are crafty with levels of acceptance and test the waters. Life simply isn't fair. There are many inequities, injustices and disproportionalities that you will face. Whether intentional or not, there will be things that happen to you and things that you do that won't complement everyone simultaneously. Sometimes you have to compromise and sometimes you have to accept what you cannot change. To that point, you need to understand what you can and cannot control. Always strive to make the best of all situations within your power, and if you don't have the power to make a positive reality for everyone then do what your heart is telling you is right.

The comprehension of ethics demands an understanding of relativity. Learn to play the game of others' ethical aptitudes, whether it is work ethics or moral ethics. If you can tap into the intelligence and the abilities of others, you will be able to identify your boundaries.

Exercises & Action Items

1. Be a good person.
2. Live in the truth.

Implied Abilities

To internalize other's motives | To choose between the lesser of evils | To attempt to find constructive solutions for all stakeholders | To be true | To have high moral standards | To communicate

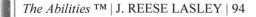

Chapter 15 | Communication

"To effectively communicate, we must realize that we are all different in the ways we perceive the world and use this understanding as a guide to our communication with others." — *Tony Robbins*

Communication is the most applicable word in our known language. The ability to communicate is imperative. If we cannot communicate we cannot exist. All living creatures have their own filters by which they interact. This can make communicating a blessing or a curse. We must tune into our own and others' senses and use them to the best of our abilities to communicate effectually.

Our human consciousness of touch, taste, feelings, sight, hearing, thinking, smelling and doing are the means to a purposeful life. These are all traits, learned and/or instinctual, that are essential to relationships, leadership and your effectiveness. Keep in mind that everyone is different and sees the world separately.

In the information age that we live in today, people are bombarded with data and information constantly. The number of thoughts that any given person has in a day are astronomical. Everyone is trying to communicate and be heard. Therefore, learn how to communicate, excellently. There are many different ways to communicate. This includes email correspondence, letters, verbal techniques, texting, touch, feelings, non-verbal insinuations, listening, understanding, flyers, memos, books, etc. Each method has its own place and time, and each one can be perceived differently, misconstrued or have a different impression, depending on the eye of the beholder.

Be a chameleon. Chameleons are masters of changing how they communicate depending upon their environment. They change their colors to blend into their habitat. They don't just approach the world with their own behavior, but also with the understanding of how others observe them. Their survival depends on their ability to adapt and communicate *the right* message.

Learn to change the way you communicate information into the world and try to understand the way the world receives that information. Perspective is important. Understand your audience. Think before you communicate and try to see through the eyes of the person you are trying to convey the message to. The impact you have on others is not as much of "what" you communicate as much as it is "how" you communicate. For example, you can say the same exact words five hundred times and get completely different reactions every time depending on how you say it. You may intend to communicate a point only to have it perceived completely different.

Learn to listen. Feedback is the most effective way to portray what you understand. Take the time to reflect on someone else's point and show the other person you respect and really hear what they are saying. It is so important to have a consensus, or common kinship, when cooperating with others.

You want to get other people to agree with you. Learn positive psychology. This is the power of "yes." You will get much further in your dealings with people if they think you respect and agree with what they are saying. If you are a constant negator, people will disagree with you and all your motives, even if your objective is correct. Also, instead of focusing on others' inabilities, focus on their abilities. People will like you for focusing on the positive and acknowledging their strengths.

Also, don't be the person who is always "one-upping" people. Even if you have better qualifications, accomplishments or credentials, you don't need to prove it. People need to feel that what they are communicating is important. If you demean them, you will lose quality interaction. People will remember the way you make them feel. If you can communicate in a way that satisfies a desire or need then you can be an inspiration to others. Also, you should only praise in public, and criticize in private. If you hurt others publicly they will shut down the lines of communication. If you need to correct someone, do it tactfully. The only way you should seem to be looking down on someone is if you are communicating that you want to help them up.

Communication is especially important in times of adversity or when you are in the midst of making ethical decisions. If you do not communicate well with people in these times, they will start to play defense, which could multiply the amount of ethical decisions you have to make. If you are in an unfortunate situation, the worst thing that you can do is to clam up or not take responsibility to communicate the issues. These are the times where remaining professional, staying unemotional and providing solutions will keep people wanting to work with you.

So, what is it that differentiates the successful communicators from the unsuccessful? Successful communicators are precise, simple, repeatable and memorable. They are able to get their point across. They bridge the gap between the stakeholders. They are intentional and relevant. Successful communicators are also the ones who listen to the needs of whomever they are interacting with. Effective communication goes both ways. The unsuccessful communicators, on the other hand, are those who do not understand their audience, over-communicate, have a narrow approach to communication methods, do not have a clear and concise message, or cannot relate. These folks suffer in their shared economy, sociology, and their EQ.

Exercises & Action Items

1. Learn how to communicate excellently.
2. Understand the methods and means of communication.
3. Learn to listen.
4. Understand your audience.
5. Change communication tactics per the environment.
6. Be simple, clear and concise.

Implied Abilities

To attune to senses | To listen | To understand | To get a point across | To be clear and concise | To relate | To avoid failure

Chapter 16 | Failing

"It is impossible to live without failing at something. Unless you live so cautiously that you might as well not have lived at all, in which case you have failed by default." — *J.K. Rowling*

There is a misconception about failure. People believe that failure is the opposite of success. However, contrary to popular belief, failure is actually a predecessor to success. The more failures you endure, the closer you get to your goal.

There are two types of people that fail. If you can compartmentalize the characteristic traits of these folks and accept them for what they are, you can choose not to live by these philosophies and to not let them hinder your ability to succeed:

1. The first is the fear of failure. People are so scared to fail that they never even try. They demean and demoralize themselves, come up with excuses for why they can't do something

or why they are not good enough. They live life by never reaching or striving or attempting. They prejudge what the outcome could be. They are negative and despondent people, in general.

2. The second is faintness of heart. These people forget, they stop trying or they get beaten down. They give up. They lose faith and hope. They believe their result is inevitable. They let past failures discourage them. They choose to not overcome. These people let their failures determine who they are instead of making their failures a part of their success. They remember the hurt of their past failures and get frightened by the thought of the worst, so they give up what could be the best. The passion was never there, their reason "why" wasn't strong enough or the pain became too overbearing.

These two kinds of people are guaranteed to fail! Exclamation mark! Success is a choice; you have to choose to win.

Success comes to those who take the chance and endure the longest, especially through failure. You have to realize that failure can actually enable you to succeed if you let it. Failure is not permanent. You should never let failure stop you. Just because you failed doesn't mean you won't succeed again. You always will have more chances, more shots, other ways and another try. Just don't quit. Just because something doesn't work the way you envisioned it, or someone or something comes in the way of your success, that doesn't define you as "unsuccessful." That only gives you a way to learn lessons, improve, change and rise to the challenge of being a better you.

Everyone faces trials, tribulations, setbacks, hardships and speed bumps in their life, but it is not the occurrence that determines their character. It is what they do with it and how they move forward that does. So, fail frequently and fail forward.

All of the greatest revolutionists of our society have failed and have seen others fail many times in their life. Take Abraham Lincoln, for example.

President Lincoln faced extreme hardship in his life. He was defeated for the state legislature, failed in business, had nervous breakdowns, was defeated for speaker, defeated for nomination to Congress, lost renomination, was rejected for land officer, was defeated for the U.S. Senate, was defeated for nomination for vice president, and was defeated for the U.S. Senate a second time. All of this happened before he became the president of the United States of America and one of the most legendary leaders of all time. If Mr. Lincoln had had the characteristics of the two types of people just mentioned, he would be nobody. He would not be written down in history and you would not have ever known about him.

What set Abraham Lincoln apart was two things: 1. He knew he would miss 100% of the chances he never took. And 2. He had endurance. He never quit. He was relentless. When the times got tough, he got tougher.

Learn to overcome. The ability to overcome will get you further than 99% of the people out there. You can let failure abolish you or you can choose to use failure to succeed. The only one that can help you is you — and you know that. Nobody is going to do it for you, so figure out a way. Let your struggle become strength, make your fear afraid of you and allow your stumble to become a stepping stone. The greater the obstacle the greater the glory in overcoming it. Reach deep inside, remember your passion, hold on to your vision and keep going.

Set boundaries. If something continually does not act in your best interest and causes you to fail, then figure out a way to change it and place boundaries to alleviate it. Setting boundaries is imperative. After you gain enough experience, you begin to recognize patterns — what does and does not work, and what is good and bad. The more you do something the more measurable it becomes. The definition of insanity is doing the exact same thing over and over and over, while each time, expecting different results. It is okay to expect different results if you modify your approach and change a variable in the equation. But never accept continual failure. You should place boundaries on the things that hurt you or have the potential to hurt you, but be creative with ways to finding alternative solutions to succeed.

Sometimes learning the hard way is needed, but the easy way is preferred. Be intelligent with how you fail, how you measure your failure, the frequency of failure, and how you choose to use your failure to change your approach to reach what you want.

Exercises & Action Items

1. Don't be afraid to fail, else you will fail.
2. Don't be faint of heart.
3. Be relentless.
4. Fail frequently and fail forward.
5. Set appropriate boundaries.
6. Keep trying and modifying your approach.

Implied Abilities

To find success | To try | To choose to win | To face trials and tribulations | To take a chance | To learn to set boundaries | To understand law, grace and mercy

Chapter 17 | Law, Grace & Mercy

"I have always found that mercy bears richer fruits than strict justice." — *Abraham Lincoln*

All have fallen short of the glory. There are more than 7 billion people on this earth today — and not even one of them is perfect. No one in history, except for Jesus himself, has proven to be fair and just in every moment. Their grandeur is tarnished to one degree or another. Everyone has a vice. All have logs in their own eye, and no one reserves the right to throw a stone. Everyone fails at some point. Everybody sins.

In the midst of the chaos and immorality of this world there are many imperfections that arise and will never cease arising. There will always be conflicts of interest, trials, disputes, arguments, unfavorable sequencing of events, disagreements, mistakes, failures and room for improvement.

When negative events occur, people experience uncomfortable feelings such as jealousy, anger, sadness, hate, resentment, guilt and fear. These feelings are very indicative that something is wrong. Recognize these feelings and use them as your internal compass to steer you away from what caused them. Pain is temporary. Everything happens for a reason. How you work through the pain will determine your character.

In the previous chapter titled "Adversity," I discussed the three different theories on conflict: avoidance, inevitableness and perpetration. I stated that each has its own place and time. One thing to understand is that in each of these applications, there can be very different impacts on the participants, depending on the law, grace or mercy extended.

You need to learn to work with people, and not against them. Obtain the ability to understand their human nature and realize that people make mistakes. The goal is helping people improve and finding the most constructive (not destructive) path forward. In other words, appreciate that people are not perfect and think of the best way to help them progress. Don't lose sight of this through your and others' imperfections. Don't quit on people.

To further elucidate this point, you have a choice during these times of adversity. You can choose to exercise law, or exercise grace and mercy. Law, grace and mercy are very different, yet work hand in hand. Without law we wouldn't appreciate the grace and mercy, and without grace and mercy we wouldn't respect the law.

Law: Law is the application of a penalty paid for sin. It is conditional and grounded on what you do that causes a particular outcome. It is a binding or custom practice, justice, rule or ritual. It is the moral code written in black and white for what is good and evil.

Grace: Grace is not deserved. It is also not earned. Grace is a gift. It is an extension of patience and trust through our imperfect human nature.

Mercy: Mercy is the sparing of the harm or punishment one deserves for sin. Similar to grace, it is not earned; however, it is deserved. It is the moment one is given another chance, even though everything points to guilt.

Grace and mercy are two of the greatest gifts from God. For clarification, they are two very different things and important to distinguish. The difference between the two is that grace is the gift of freedom from penalty when we don't deserve it, while mercy is forgiveness from the penalty when we do deserve it. For example, grace is not punishing a baby for crying; mercy is not punishing a man who chose to commit murder. Grace involves unconscious and unpreventable naivety; mercy involves conscious, willing intent or conscious, reluctant action through weakness.

So, what is the difference in the ramification of penalty (or law), compared to the ramification of grace and mercy? Answer: Grace and mercy have a higher probability of creating a positive result.

Grace and mercy have the potential to help people realize their imperfections without the consequence, which leads to gratitude if they understand what the consequence could've been. Gratitude leads to a humble approach of wanting to change for the greater good and living a better life. If people can't change they feel comforted in the fact that they are forgiven and they admit shortcomings, which is the first step to recovery. The risk here is if people are given the grace and mercy, do they take the law for granted?

Law, on the other hand, forces someone to change, whether they like it or not. It causes resentment, pain and suffering. This can lead to change for the better if the penalty is stronger than the original behavior. However, law has the potential to cause even more sin. The person has a harder time letting go of their pride and if they can't change, they either resort to living a lie, hiding or feeling inadequate. They keep others from the truth because they fear the consequence of the truth.

Extending grace and mercy is easier said than done. Forgiveness is challenging, yet so freeing. Divine justice is much different than justice meted out by a civil society. Jesus teaches us in Matthew 5:43, "Love your enemies, bless those who curse you and forgive those who hurt you." But what about the repeat offenders? In Matthew 18:21-35 (NIV), Jesus teaches us "The Parable of the Unmerciful Servant."

21 Then Peter came to Jesus and asked, "Lord, how many times shall I forgive my brother or sister who sins against me? Up to seven times?"

22 Jesus answered, "I tell you, not seven times, but seventy times seven times.

23 Therefore, the kingdom of heaven is like a king who wanted to settle accounts with his servants.

24 As he began the settlement, a man who owed him ten thousand bags of gold was brought to him.

25 Since he was not able to pay, the master ordered that he and his wife and his children and all that he had be sold to repay the debt.

26 At this the servant fell on his knees before him. 'Be patient with me,' he begged, 'and I will pay back everything.'

27 The servant's master took pity on him, canceled the debt and let him go.

28 But when that servant went out, he found one of his fellow servants who owed him a hundred silver coins. He grabbed him and began to choke him. 'Pay me back what you owe me!' he demanded.

29 His fellow servant fell to his knees and begged him, 'Be patient with me, I will pay it back.'

30 But he refused. Instead, he went off and had the man thrown into prison until he could pay the debt.

31 When the other servants saw what had happened, they were outraged and went and told their master everything that had happened.

32 Then the master called the servant in. 'You wicked servant,' he said, 'I canceled all that debt of yours because you begged me to.

33 Shouldn't you have had mercy on your fellow servant just as I had on you?'

34 In anger his master handed him over to the jailers to be tortured, until he should pay back all he owed.

35 This is how my heavenly Father will treat each of you unless you forgive your brother or sister from your heart."

Sin is very deceiving. It actually creates more sin and causes a downward spiral. This is no way to live! We must charge forward with defeating these evils. We must nip these events and feelings in the bud before they become irrevocable disasters.

No matter who you are, or where you come from, you will need grace and mercy at some point in your life. So does everyone else. Everyone needs a helping hand or a leg up at some point in their life. Everyone is on their own journey.

The wise man learns the easy way through understanding consequence without having to experience it. The fool has to hit rock bottom before he changes. Don't let others' corruption corrupt you. Stand firm in your righteousness and extend mercy often.

Exercises & Action Items

1. Appreciate others' and your own imperfections.
2. Find the most constructive way to improve.
3. Choose to extend mercy often.

Implied Abilities

To comprehend the results of sin | To know what is right and wrong | To feel good | To forgive | To give more chances | To not judge | To be just | To learn improvement and excellence

Chapter 18 | Improving & Excellence

"We are what we repeatedly do. Excellence therefore, is not an act, but a habit." — *Aristotle*

The pursuit of excellence is constant, living and dynamic, and there is always room for improvement. There is no ceiling in the room for improvement; it is endless. Whether you are recognizing your need to change because you are experiencing conflict, or if you are the greatest in the world at what you do, there are always areas to advance and progress. Set forth the expectation of yourself to always continue to learn and grow.

Beware of stagnation. If you stop moving, absorbing, flowing and thirsting, you will become lifeless. The essence of a good quality of life is newness, production and cultivation. A barren desert is to a meandering river as stagnation is to excellence.

Excellence is not being the best; it is *always* doing your best and trying your hardest to be a better you. There is a significant difference between knowing excellence and doing excellence. You can recognize when someone is excellent, but being the person who is excellent is a different story. Do excellence.

There are two superlative words that depict excellence: kaizen and auspicious.

Kaizen: A Japanese philosophy meaning "continuous improvement"

Auspicious: Characterized by success

Challenge yourself to not live by the confines of the status quo. Be better. I call this having the case of the "ers". Bigg*er*, fast*er*, strong*er*, smart*er*, long*er*, happi*er*, wealthi*er*, healthi*er*... whatev*er* is bett*er*. Learn to raise the bar and then raise it again. Keep breaking records, continually discover, overturn the next rock, measure and analyze, find innovative solutions, create value, modify techniques and push your limits.

One of the greatest examples of someone who portrayed this behavior and lived life to the fullest, was Walter Payton. "Sweetness," as they called him, was an American football running back who played in the NFL for the Chicago Bears and was arguably the best back that ever played the game. He was a record breaker and a history maker. He played for thirteen seasons and had a total of 16,726 rushing yards, 125 total touchdowns, 492 career receptions, and 77 one-hundred-yard games. He was elected into the Pro Football Hall of Fame in 1993. He was the best at what he did, held record after record, was always challenging himself and others around him, always improved — and he did it with humility.

The key to developing a quality and purposeful life is having the ability to reflect on your past to in order to leverage the present so that you may change the future in a positive way. If you do not have a basis from which to measure, you cannot track your progress. This is why it is so important to set realistic SMARTER goals (from Chapter One), baseline them and frequently check your progress as you advance toward them. You know yourself better than anyone else, so find ways to constantly help yourself by being your own constructive critic. You should learn to make advancement a ritual. Place qualitative and quantitative measures on your behaviors and outcomes.

When you reach important milestones in your life make it a point to spend time to notice and record your lessons learned and best practices. Figure out what worked and what didn't work. Deeply examine what the reasons were for your success or failure. Reflect on the events and circumstances, and then make the effort to log or journal your growth stages.

Your ability to be educated through retaining and applying information will be the most profound enabler of your development. Be a computer. A computer, as an analogy, has a hard drive that stores all of the information (your brain capacity) and a processor to extrapolate the data to produce information over a given time (your memory and cognitive skills). The bigger the hard drive and the faster the processor, the more you will expedite your erudition curve and capitalize on opportunity to improve.

Once you have identified the causes of your wins or losses and memorialized their characteristics, then you can be creative with ways to provide more value.

Exercises & Action Items

1. Continuously improve and always look for ways to add value.
2. Create lessons learned and best practices at your milestones.
3. Celebrate your accomplishments along the way.

Implied Abilities

To advance | To progress | To do your best | To continually become better | To defeat the status quo | To break records | To retain information | To process information | To learn lessons | To portray faith, hope and love

Chapter 19 | Faith, Hope & Love

"And now these three remain: faith, hope, and love, but the greatest of these is love."
— *1 Corinthians 13:13*

Of all the abilities mentioned in this book, none reach the echelon of faith, hope and love. They are intertwined in everything you do and they are the energy for all abilities. Faith and hope have propelled you to where you are. Love is the reason why you did it.

Faith, hope and love are the beginning and the end. With them you have purpose. Without them you never would have had the desire or the vision in the first place. You wouldn't have acted on your dream. You never would've changed. You would've been stagnant. You never would have had to manage your risk because you never would've had the audacity to take the risk. At no time would you have earned anything because there would be nothing worth earning.

Needless to say, you never would have overcome adversity or learned the value of integrity. You never would have acquired and managed resources to reach your goal. Your portfolio would not be as diversified. You never would have comprehended the meaning of ethics or learned to communicate effectively. You never would have grown from failure. You wouldn't understand the difference between law, grace and mercy. You wouldn't have aimed for improvement or excellence. You wouldn't have anything to balance. What reward would you have? What could you give back? There would be a slight impact, but no legacy. In other words, what have you if you have not faith, hope and love? They are the root and the fruit.

Faith: Faith is trust. Faith is ability to believe in what is yet to be manifested. It is the moment of opportunity when you make a decision to follow your desire. Faith is knowing anything can be done. Miracles happen when faith is apparent and faith is confirmed by the miracles. It is the belief that helps you take the first step and gives you the ability to figure it out along the way. Belief is more powerful than technical aptitude. If you believe you can do something, it is achievable. Faith will give you the belief, belief will give you the ability to try and trying will help you solve the technicalities.

Hope: Hope is holding onto positive expectations. It is knowing that there is something better. It is assurance. It is the overcoming of fear and all resistance. It is encouragement. It is strengthening. It is the moment when you are dealing with uncertainty but continue to fight the battle. It is the foundation of the mission and the purpose. It is the seeking of the end goal. It is the ability to see there is light even through all the darkness. Hope is like a connection of tunnels that lead to the opening of a new world, a new reality.

Love: Love, over everything else is the greatest and ultimate ability. Love is the common denominator and the underlying universal truth. Love is giving yourself to others and accepting them for who they are. Love is the most profound word in our common language. Love itself can be a language. Love is giving. Love is charity. Love is creation. Love does not judge. Love does not hide. Love sustains. Love provides. Love is empathy. Love is caring. Love is the best intentions. Love is happiness. Love is compassion. Love is sacrifice for the greater good. Love is purity. Love is everything that is good.

1 Corinthians 13: 4-8 describes love this way: "Love is patient, love is kind. It does not envy, it does not boast, it is not proud. It does not dishonor others, it is not self-seeking, it is not easily angered, it keeps no record of wrongs. Love does not delight in evil but rejoices with the truth. It always protects, always trusts, always hopes, always perseveres. Love never fails." John 15:13 depicts the greatest love this way: "There is no greater love than to lay down one's life for one's friends." You see, love, after all, matters the most.

Where these abilities are worthy and the most honorable, they also are the most challenging to achieve. These values are not for the faint of heart.

Faith, hope and love are much easier said than done. People have a challenging time with these. They get stuck in their ways, they get negative or they give up. Adversity overcomes the power of the blessings.

People often overlook their reason why. They lose their desire, forget their vision. They choose to not excel and improve, and don't accomplish what they set out for. They get hurt and then they choose to not use their abilities to grow. Instead, their quality of life declines.

Life is hard sometimes. Things are complex and dynamic. Nobody said it was easy. However, if people are able to uphold faith, hope and love, their lives hold virtue.

To draw an analogy, faith, hope and love are like driving a vehicle. In order for that car to get to where it needs to go, you need to start the car, put it in gear and give it the energy source to move such a large mass. There are a lot of mechanisms that need to work together to get that car to move, but without the gas there is no movement, no power. As the car accelerates, more power is needed. There also are more risks and dangers along the way. You will face many dynamic forces.   There are speed bumps, signs to different places, other people driving, weather and so forth. Life happens. You need to work with these things and use proper driving techniques to accomplish your goal. If you don't have enough gas you won't get there. You need to find the gas stations along the way to refuel your purpose and mission.

Ultimately, if you are able to keep driving, you get to where you want to go. When you look back you realize that love was the reason to go somewhere. Your faith and hope helped you figure it out. Without faith, hope and love, you wouldn't have gotten there.

So, what drives you? What keeps you going? What got you going in the first place? What is your fuel, your source of power? What helps you overcome? Where are you going and why are you going there?

Do it out of love, keep the faith, and hold onto hope.

Exercises & Action Items

1. Do everything you do with love.
2. Use the energy of faith and hope when life gets tough.
3. Focus on your sources of positivity and purity.

Implied Abilities

To hunt | To seek | To pursue | To understand sozo | To have best intentions | To be pure | To see the light | To have positive expectations | To continue | To retain | To agree | To find balance & health

Chapter 20 | Balance & Health

"Step with care and great tact, and remember that
life's a balancing act." — *Dr. Seuss*

There is a lot that goes into an excellent quality of
life. Throughout your journey of achieving what you
want, you need to be able to keep things in
perspective. Life is complex and you may have many
aspirations you are working toward simultaneously,
some of which could conflict with each other.

Imagine your quality of life as an upside-down
triangle. This triangle is *balancing* on a foundation of
your means of life that you have built. Your life
includes qualities such as those that are spiritual,
physical, physiological, sociological, emotional and
financial. Your foundation is made up of all the
"bricks of life", such as family, friends, animals, work,
your home, your career, your transportation, your
potential, and other factors important to you. Your
foundation must be a system of stability or else your

quality of life will lose balance and fall. All the bricks must be placed and adhered together delicately in the system. If one of them cracks or falls out of place, the things that matter the most could be at risk.

Ask yourself what is important to your quality of life. Organize things in such a manner that you can achieve what you want without giving something up. If you do not have a balance, something will eventually break. You need to find what keeps you happy and gives you purpose. Then juggle everything while understanding what matters most. In other words, you have to find an equilibrium with your portfolio of initiatives. Each has its own special needs. You need to foster each in its own environment and give each one what it needs to grow.

There are opportunity costs associated with all of your wants. For example, you may have a wonderful business opportunity to make a fortune but if you work so hard you that you have a heart attack — you can lose everything. You may love to travel but if it consumes your family time — your kids could lose critical interactions with you in their developmental stages. You may have a job that gets you by, but if you are unhappy, is it worth it? You get the point.

Strive to be well-rounded at the same time as being effective. While you want to strive to be multifaceted, you need to ensure you are also accomplished. An over-accumulation of tasks could cause some of your bricks to bear unnecessary forces.

Don't sacrifice what you really want for what you want right now. The worst thing that can happen is to inflict catastrophe on an important quality of life aspect in order to achieve another. This will make your foundation weak and you will end up lacking the strength to hold those bricks together, inevitably sacrificing your desires.

There is a strong connection between being balanced and being healthy. In other words, having a good quality of life and being healthy are one in the same. It is the wellspring to living a purposeful life. The greatest wealth is health. It is a priceless possession, so take good care of it. It is an all-encompassing ability that enables you to achieve further abilities. Health embraces the mind, body and spirit. The mind, body and spirit can sharpen or fade. You need to cherish and honor all three. They each can impact the others.

We are imperfect beings. Illness can happen because of what we do and because of what happens to us. You need to do everything and anything you can to stay healthy, prevent illness and continually heal. That can mean eating right, praying, meditating, exercising, laughing, avoiding drugs, reading, being happy, feeling peace, brushing your gums, cleaning out your belly button, you name it. Unhealthy habits will catchup to you and you will regret it. They will prohibit your ability to succeed in one way, shape, form or another. Don't become enslaved and addicted to injurious behaviors that prohibit your freedom. It is also important to live in moderation; too much of one thing could be detrimental to your purpose.

Let's take stress for example. Beware of stress. You can become tired, overwhelmed, unproductive, reactive, upset, scared and it could even lead to a nervous breakdown, cancer, or a heart attack. Too much stress can wear down the mind, body and spirit. This is unhealthy.

Another great example is promiscuity. If you get caught up in this, your heart can be forgotten. Turning love to lust leads to nothing more than wasted resources, illness, jealousy, deceit and broken promises.

There are many examples of things you should and shouldn't do. But to get the point across, being unhealthy is like holding up your jacket by its sleeve. If you hold your jacket this way things will naturally fall out, making a mess. But if you hold your jacket by the middle of the collar, that way, everything is organized and just falls into place.

It is worthy to note that there is no "one size fits all" proposition when it comes to balance and health. Each person has their own unique situation, environment and phases. Define priority, know your limits, set boundaries and place appropriate timelines while walking the tightrope of life.

Exercises & Action Items

1. Build a sturdy foundation.
2. Uphold your desires by balancing everything without compromising anything.
3. Be fit.

Implied Abilities

To keep things in perspective | To work on multiple goals simultaneously | To build a foundation | To not burn out | To have priorities | To be well-rounded | To be healthy | To not impede | To live in moderation | To know your limits | To get what you want without giving something up | To get your reward

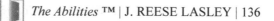

Chapter 21 | Reward

"I do not choose to be a common man. It is my right to be uncommon — if I can. I seek opportunity — not security. I do not wish to be a kept citizen, humbled and dulled by having the State look after me. I want to take the calculated risk, to dream and to build. To fail and to succeed. I refuse to barter incentive for a dole; I prefer the challenges of life to the guaranteed existence; the thrill of fulfillment to the stale calm of Utopia. I will not trade freedom for beneficence, nor my dignity for a handout. I will never cower before any master, nor bend to any threat. It is my heritage to stand erect, proud and unafraid; to think and act for myself, to enjoy the benefit of my creations, and to face the world boldly and say: This, with God's help, I have done. All this is what it means to be an Entrepreneur." — *Thomas Paine*

Great Job! You made it! You worked hard for this. You have realized what you set out to achieve. You are the master of your intention. You have carried your mission and vision to fruition. You made the choice to grow and to live life to the fullest. This is one of those moments to be grateful for. This is one of those moments that you will look back on and feel proud of, I guarantee it.

Take a second to embrace what is worthy of praise. Honor where you have been and remember this special feeling of success. Look at everything you have learned along the way, the relationships you have created and the resources you have attained.

There is something to be said about the person who can see something through. While out hiking to the top of a mountain, a great friend and mentor of mine, Stephen Pettis, once told me something I will never forget. He said, "If you put one foot in front of the other, one day you will look and see you have done something incredible." This analogy and these inspirational words resonated with me. Let them do so for you as well.

While it is important to strive for the future, do not forget the importance of living in the moment by appreciating your fruits and blessings. Do something significant to recognize the reward. It is so important to celebrate your accomplishments along the way. Those accreditations and merits will act as encouragers.

This is an exciting day because of everything you have accomplished and also because of everywhere you are about to be going. Remember, excellence is a journey, not a destination. Once you find those things that work and make it worth it, you can stick to them and then build upon them.

Your life just doesn't stop here. Use this day as leverage to get yourself to the next level — and continue living your life to the fullest!

Always remember, success is a journey of getting what you want and, more importantly, feeling proud of it when you get there.

This is the first day of the rest of your life!

Exercises & Action Items

1. Celebrate your accomplishments.
2. Be grateful and appreciate life and all of the little moments along the way.
3. Build on what works by charging forward fearlessly to get what you want.
4. Continue to grind and eventually you will shine.

Implied Abilities

To be successful | To accomplish | To achieve | To get what you want | To celebrate | To feel proud | To continue the journey | To build upon your success | To give back

Chapter 22 | Giving Back

"The meaning of life is to find your gift. The purpose of life is to give it away." — *Pablo Picasso*

Remarkably, there is only one thing that is actually more rewarding than the reward itself — and that's giving back. Just as reproduction is the key to life, so is re-creation to success.

Imagine yourself as an apple tree. When we started this journey you had just planted your seed. Overtime, as you grew, your roots spread and you built your groundwork. You found your nutrients and eventually you sprouted with substance. You grew more, experienced your environment and when the season was right, you began to bloom. *Eventually*, you produced fruit. These fruits and blessings now have given you the ability of mission and purpose from which the world (and also you) can benefit from.

There are many different types of trees and many different types of fruits. Different trees offer different blessings. Every one is unique. Gifts are wonderful. Gifts are positive. They are recognized by peace, happiness, growth, patience, kindness, gentleness and love. So, I ask you, what fruit do you bear and how are you identified by it? How do you contribute value to the world? How can you (and do you) give back?

Just because you nail an apple to a fencepost, doesn't mean that it is a fruit tree. Even though it meets the requirements of wood in the ground and it is holding up fruit, it is missing one important thing — the ability to reproduce. The continuance of giving is necessary to your growth and your growth is necessary to your giving.

If you are not growing you're dying. Therefore, give the gift of giving. We have all heard the saying that you can give a horse some water and fulfill its thirst, but if you lead a horse to water, you will help it drink for a lifetime.

Let's rephrase this differently. Imagine yourself as the earth's water supply. Realize how it cycles. There are underground aquifers that feed creeks, which flow into rivers, which along the way create ponds and lakes, and ultimately run into the ocean. On its way there, the water evaporates and creates rain and snow, and it supplies all of the creatures of creation with a necessary ingredient, or gift, to live: water. The trees, the plants, the animals, the insects — they all use this gift and have their purpose, too. Every living creature gives back in its own unique way. Buffalo will till the ground so that it is aerated. Bees will spread pollen from flower to flower. Plants will create oxygen. You get the point. The cycle recycles. So, what life do you support? How do you flow to others?

You see, the more you grow, earn and produce, the more you realize that you need everyone and everything else around you (and vice versa). If you cooperate with others, others will cooperate with you.

What you will find is that it is much more blessed to give than it is to receive. Giving back, in return, gives you back the gift of graciousness. Not only do you feel good about having the ability to help others, but you learn more in the process, which gains you more than you would have by just achieving your goal. In other words, the most fulfilling thing you can do once you get what you want is to show someone else how to get it. Leverage your newly acquired skills and resources to help others achieve what they want. It continues the cycle.

You will get what you give. If you look back on your journey of earning, you will find you gave first and then received later, and continue to do so. You gave first, then reaped the reward second. While you are giving, help others realize they shouldn't just focus on the getting. They too should focus on the giving. The people who focus on the getting are unhappy. They forget the cycle and halt the circle of life. The people who focus on giving create change. The goal is to start off giving more than you take — and end up giving more than you take. Grow.

You know better than anyone else about what it took to get what you wanted. You had the aspiration, you had the vision and you had the drive. You took the action and figured out how to get there. You were the one who defeated the status quo and overcame the obstacles. There is no one else on earth with your experience and no one better positioned to offer insight. Your unique approach and knowledge have now afforded you the opportunity to take your gifts and give them forward.

Ask yourself how you can "reciprocate" to society, your environment or an individual. What would that really entail?

First, you need to soul-search and identify what your gifts truly are. Reflect on your life and notice your natural and learned abilities. Specify your strengths. Then, figure out their value and purpose for helping others.

Secondly, you need select your recipient. This is a necessary element in giving. You need to be careful with whom you choose to give to and how you go about it. People can try to take advantage of you, and if you give without making people earn, you defeat the purpose of giving at all. You will actually *take away*.

Find the person who not only wants what you have but is willing to work for it and give back. Also, find the person who would appreciate the gift and would grow with it.

Third, you need to be a coach. You need to guide them through attaining success. Their journey may look and feel differently than yours. They may have different resources, different drive, different aspirations and so forth. Even if your gift to others is not exactly what you achieved yourself, there are many gifts that can stem from your success. Therefore, offer up your teachings where it relates and can expedite their learning curve.

Finally, encourage them and be a beacon of hope. Help them realize the end goal. Support them and keep giving what you have to give. After all, you were the success story. You were the testimony of faith. So, stand strong and offer excitement and anticipation.

Giving is the secret to continuing success and achieving what you and others want.

Exercises & Action Items

1. Use your purpose to add success to others.
2. Give the gift of giving.
3. Continuously give — and don't ever stop giving.

Implied Abilities

To reproduce | To re-create | To produce fruit | To have mission and purpose | To recycle | To support life | To reciprocate | To choose a recipient | To teach | To testify | To leave an impact | To be a legacy

Chapter 23 | Impact & Legacy

"How can I help the greatest number of people in the greatest way?" — *Gary Tuerak, President of the National Society of Leadership and Success*

We started this book with imagining you were lying on your deathbed, reflecting on your life and everything that transpired. The sweet times, the sad times, the shameful times, the happy times, your first kiss, your first job, your best moment — all of those memories.

For whatever reason, you have kept those memories. But why!? What made it worth it to you? What were you most proud of? What were your struggles? What did you take for granted? What would you do if you had a second chance? What would you change? What gave you fulfillment? What did you live for?

In retrospect, now that you have achieved your desire and reached important milestones on your journey, it is important to reflect on how you have improved, how you have touched the lives of others, what sort of footprint you left along your journey and how you have impacted the world.

Impact is the moment when someone grasps the understanding that you have affected them. Legacy is endless value (tangible or intangible), which always continues to provide blessings to a person, an organization or the environment.

So, how big did you dream? How far was your reach? How did you influence your reality? How did you affect your and others' quality of life? What impression did you make on others? What improved? How did you help? Was it worthwhile? Did it provide value? Was it meaningful? What did you leave behind? How will people remember you? Were you successful? Were you auspicious? What was your mark on the world?

Whether you are aware of it or not, you left an imprint. Your footprints left a trail of your character and your fingerprints presented their own unique appeal. You left a mark. But to what degree? Was your mark remarkable?

See, perception is everything. People can construe your mark in an infinite amount of ways. All that you can strive for is that you are thought of highly, your reputation is honorable and your application continues. Have you ever heard that saying, "Everything they touch turns to gold"? That's what you want people to think about you. If people feel grateful when they look at what you did for them, then you have touched their lives. If the system or memories you made continue to bring blessings, even after you are gone, then you have accomplished something extraordinary.

The more you can contribute to society and your environment in profound and valuable ways, the better. The greater the impact the greater the ripple effect. You are paid in direct proportion to the amount of peoples' lives you affect — and not in money alone, but also in blessings.

Every positive impact is important and should be honored. If you want to be great, you need to find ways to impact the masses and be remembered. They say that the average person will have a profound influence on five people's lives in their lifetime. What if you could change the world? What if you could revolutionize humanity?

Think of the Wright brothers, for example. These two brothers had a dream to fly. They pioneered one of the most revolutionary inventions of all time: the airplane. It literally changed the course of humanity. They showed people that human flight was possible. Today, over one hundred years later, we have aircraft flying all over the world. Air travel brought people convenience, reachability and lifted humankind to new heights. The brothers' legacy continues because their little idea to make a flying machine that added extraordinary value to society.

Think of Henry Bessemer, the gentleman who made mass production of steel economical. Without Henry, we wouldn't have the high-rise buildings, the railroads, the cars, the computers, all of the products that are developed with machinery and many other things we take for granted. This man helped shape the industrial age, transforming the course of history.

Think of Bill Gates and Steve Jobs. These "early adopters" helped develop the information age. Their vision of computers enabled *everyone* to live better lives through information, data, analytics, and programming. There is no better way to impact the masses than through the Internet. More than three-fourths of the billionaires on the planet have been created from the tech industry.

Where would we be without these people and others similar to them who have chosen to live a life of impact and legacy? It is amazing how so few have taken a path of remarkable impact and are able to leave a legacy on humanity.

Therefore, I challenge you to stretch your thinking. Continue the journey. Be creative with innovative ways to leave your mark on humanity. Ultimately, your impact should be purposeful, positive and powerful, and your legacy should be one of relentless giving. This is what makes it worth it. This is what you work so hard for. This is your reason why.

In summary, this is your life, your purpose. It is unique and it is your own. You can achieve what you want. This is the first day of the rest of your life, so go live it to the best of your abilities.

Exercises & Action Items

1. Reflect on how you have affected others.
2. Be a positive remembrance.
3. Change the world and humanity.

Implied Abilities

To make memories | To not burden | To continue blessings | To make a positive difference | To affect | To leave your mark

Conclusion

Everybody wants something. Everybody is going after it with the best of their abilities. But do they really have the abilities to get what they want?

There are many definitions, insights and interpretations of success. People have different perceptions of what they believe success means. They spend their whole live striving for money, quality time, happiness, ways to help others, a respectable job, a better role, a family, heaven, freedom, health, a big house, a nice car, friends, or whatever is important to them. Success, in its fundamental construct, is simple. It is really just getting what you want.

The problem is that many people don't really know what they want. Of those people who do know *what* they want, many don't know *why* they want it or *how* to get it — or even believe they can have it.

Whatever it is that you want to improve your quality of life, you can get it. You can do it. You have

The Abilities. In other words, this book defines the abilities to help you get what you want, from desire to legacy

... Now, let's go get it!

About the Author

J. Reese Lasley is an avid entrepreneur, visionary, life coach and business consultant. He is the founder of The Abilities LLC, an organization that provides individuals and businesses with the abilities to be successful. He provides a strong, clear, true, authentic and empowering message of positivity, purity, faith, courage, wisdom, love and creation. With his faith-based self-help approach, he guides people through the path of attaining what they desire and supports them with realizing their full potential.